the CROPS WE GROW

GEORGIA AMSON-BRADSHAW

New York

This edition published in 2020 by Cavendish Square Publishing, LLC
243 5th Avenue, Suite 136, New York, NY 10016

First Edition

Website: cavendishsq.com

Cataloging-in-Publication Data
Names: Amson-Bradshaw, Georgia.
Title: The crops we grow / Georgia Amson-Bradshaw.
Description: New York : Cavendish Square Publishing, 2020. | Series: Eco STEAM | Includes glossary and index.
Identifiers: ISBN 9781502649072 (pbk.) | ISBN 9781502648983 (library bound) | ISBN 9781502649058 (ebook)
Subjects: LCSH: Sustainable agriculture--Juvenile literature. | Food-supply--Environmental aspects--Juvenile literature.
Classification: LCC S494.5.S86 A56 2020 | DDC 631.5--dc23

Picture acknowledgements:
Images from Shutterstock.com: jsp 4t, Standret 4b, hoang thai 5t, Capture_The_World 5l, kreatto 5r, Stockr 6t, Jinning Li 6b, Orn Rin 7t, JoeyPhoto 7b, Arnain 8t, LineTale 8b, mescal 9r, PixieMe 9b, LorraineHudgins 10t, Patrick Jennings 10b, Bika Ambon 11c, Efimenko Alexander 11b, Loboda Dmytro 12t, robuart 12b, Milles Studio 13t, Meryll 16, Dan Schreiber 17t, Tomacco 17b, Robert Adrian Hillman 18l, Rita Meraki 18r, Jorgen Mcleman 18b, snapgalleria 19t, Yuriy Chertok 19b, Tatiana Liubimova 20t, Robert Adrian Hillman 21t, Hennadii H 21b, images72 24t, irin-k 25t, Jack Hong 26t, udaix 26b, Pelevina Ksinia 27t, bartzdim 27b, pic0bird 28l, Sabelskaya 29t, EMJAY SMITH 29b, Gaidamashchuk 30, Cbenjasuwan 32r, Iakov Filimonov 32b, MIA Studio 33t, Kent Weakley 33b, natalia bulatova 34t, Julia_fdt 34l, Ken Schulze 34b, petovarga 36t, Karkas 37t, xieyuliang 40b, Pavel 41c, Julia_Snova 41t, Elena Koromyslova 41b, Denys Koltovskyi 42l, NEILRAS 42c, Rimma Rii 43, Designbek 44, n. yanchuk 45c, Artisticco 45b, petovarga 45t

Images from Getty: SolStock 35t, Eduardo1961 40t, kupicoo 46t, cnicbc 46b

NASA Visible Earth 11t

Illustrations on pages 15, 23, 31 and 39 by Steve Evans.

All design elements from Shutterstock.

Printed in the United States of America

CONTENTS

FARMING AROUND THE WORLD

People started farming crops many thousands of years ago. Rice was grown in China at least as far back as 11,000 BCE. Agriculture is an ancient activity which has shaped the planet, and huge areas of Earth's land are taken up with growing crops. Around the world, many different edible plants are grown in a huge variety of landscapes, using all sorts of different techniques according to local conditions and tastes.

Grain crops such as wheat and barley were important in Ancient Egypt.

In the UK, over 71 percent of the land is used for agriculture. In some countries, such as South Africa, it is over 80 percent.

Diverse technology

Farming is a far more varied activity than we might imagine. The science and technology used to grow different crops in different places is incredibly diverse. Some techniques have remained unchanged for thousands of years, whereas in other places new developments are revolutionizing how fruits, vegetables, and grains are grown.

Ancient and modern

In tropical places with steep slopes such as the Philippines, rice is grown in terraces cut into hillsides, flooded with water and then drained at harvest time. This technique has been used for thousands of years. In contrast, in Australia, new technology is being used to grow tomatoes in the desert, using solar power. Seawater is pumped in, and the salt is removed before growing tomatoes in soilless vegetable beds inside greenhouses.

Big and small

Farms vary greatly in size and the way in which they are run around the world. Globally, around 84 percent of farms are very small (less than two hectares in size, which is roughly two soccer fields). Many of them are in poorer countries and are farmed using only animals and hand tools. In well-off countries, such as the USA, farming is dominated by large farms, some of them thousands of hectares in size. On large farms, processes such as ploughing and harvesting are done by machine.

SPOTLIGHT:

SUBSISTENCE FARMERS

Subsistence farmers only grow enough food for themselves and their families on a small plot. Other farms are huge businesses, selling vast amounts of produce around the world.

Subsistence farmers grow their own food.

IMPACTS OF FARMING

Many farmers around the world are already growing food in sustainable ways. However in a lot of countries, particularly well-off places such as the USA and Europe, the way in which most crops are grown is not sustainable (meaning it can't be continued without causing severe ecological damage). This is having very serious effects on wildlife, as unsustainable farming erodes the soil and drains water supplies, while also contributing to climate change.

Unsustainable inputs

Planting the same crop year after year drains the soil of nutrients, and makes the soil weak. This means large amounts of chemical fertilizers are needed to grow crops; fertilizers that come from finite sources such as fossil fuels. Without a mixture of plants, the natural balance of plants, predators and prey that exists in an ecosystem is disrupted, and certain insect pests and weeds run rampant. This in turn means huge amounts of chemical pesticides and herbicides are needed to protect the crops. You can read more about the problems of pesticides on pages 24–25.

Pesticides are applied to a field of crops.

SPOTLIGHT: MONOCULTURE

Monoculture is where one crop, such as wheat or soya beans, is grown in a particular area – often a very large area – year after year.

soya beans

Climate change

Intensive monoculture farming contributes to climate change in several ways. Processing the fossil fuels to make fertilizers and pesticides releases greenhouse gases, which contribute to global warming, into the atmosphere. Healthy soil is a natural store of carbon, but when soils are eroded by intensive agriculture, they release the carbon back into the atmosphere. Intensive agriculture also relies on a lot of heavy machinery, such as tractors and combine harvesters, which produce a lot of greenhouse gas emissions.

Storing up problems

In a vicious circle, agriculture contributes to climate change, while climate change damages the security of our food supply by causing droughts and other unpredictable weather patterns. The same goes for soil erosion, as the yield, or the amount of crops produced on each piece of land, goes down due to poor soils. These problems in turn reduce our ability to feed the world's population.

As the world's population grows, we will need to produce more food on the same amount of land, and in a sustainable way. Read more about some specific challenges and STEAM solutions to them on the following pages.

THE ISSUE:
RAINFOREST DEFORESTATION

Tropical rainforests are one of the Earth's most amazing and important habitats. They cover just 7 percent of the Earth's surface, yet they contain over half of Earth's plant and animal species. As well as being home to many plants, animals, and people, they play a very important role in keeping the Earth habitable for everyone. The rainforests help keep global climate and rainfall in balance. They store a huge amount of carbon in their vegetation, helping to clean the air of carbon dioxide.

Warning: destruction

Deforestation is when trees and plants are cut down to clear the land. One and a half acres of rainforest around the world are cut down every second, roughly the size of one and a half soccer fields, with terrible impacts on our climate and biodiversity. Because the rainforests store so much carbon from the atmosphere, cutting and burning the rainforests is contributing around 18–20 percent of the world's carbon emissions each year, severely affecting global warming. Without the rainforests to regulate rainfall, drought will also become much more common – with deadly consequences.

We are currently on track to lose half of Earth's plant and animal species over the next 25 years.

Why clear the land?

Trees are cleared for many reasons, including mining operations, or logging for timber. But the single largest cause of deforestation is clearing land for agriculture. Much of this is to make space to graze cattle, or to grow soya beans for their feed. However some land is cleared for other cash crops. Farmers in poorer countries in Asia, Africa, and South and Central America can make a living by growing crops such as coffee beans and cocoa for chocolate, and selling them to people in developed countries, such as the UK and the USA.

SPOTLIGHT CASH CROP

A cash crop is a crop such as cocoa grown and sold for money, rather than being eaten by the farmer or grown to protect the soil.

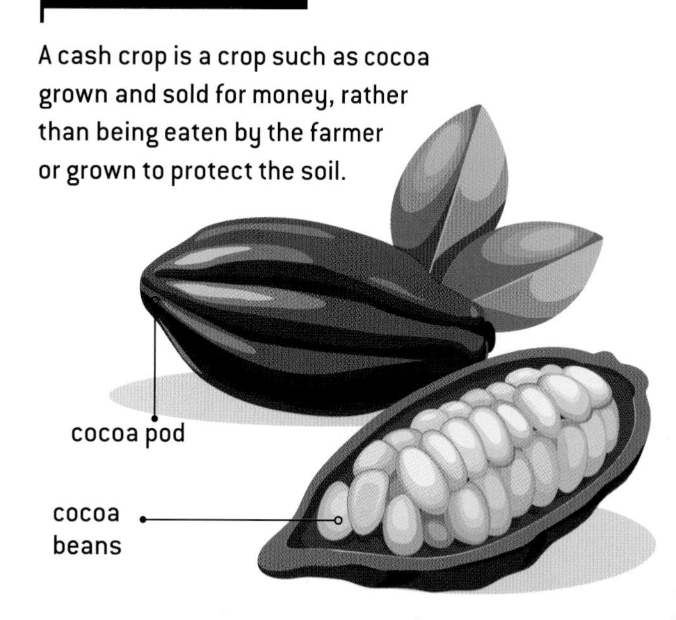

People and the planet

Although it is essential to preserve the rainforests, what should happen to the people who rely on the destruction of the rainforest to make a living? For many people in poorer countries, there is no other work available. Millions of farmers rely on people in other countries drinking coffee and eating chocolate, and getting another job isn't an option. So how can they feed their own families, while keeping the rainforest intact?

HABITAT DESTRUCTION

A habitat is a animal or a plant's home. It is the area it lives in, including the landscape made of the rocks and soil, and all the other plants and animals that live there. A living thing's habitat provides it with food, shelter, and other living things of the same type so it can reproduce.

Animal adaptations

Living things are adapted to their habitat. For example, plants on the rainforest floor are adapted to the shady, damp conditions and the rich soil. Many rainforest animals have camouflage that lets them blend in with the vegetation. Rainforest birds can build their nests in the tree canopy (the high, dense layer of branches and leaves). In addition, the population of each living thing is kept in check by predators. Everything is kept in balance. By removing the trees and plants from a rainforest, the balance is destroyed.

To our eyes, a field of crops or grass for cows might look natural compared to a road or a building, but to a forest creature it is just as impossible to live there.

Ripple effects

Damage to a habitat also has effects on other habitats and ecosystems around it. For example, large trees slow the speed at which rain reaches the ground. Removing them allows rain to run more quickly across the land and erode the soil. The soil then runs into the rivers and then eventually the sea, where it creates pollution. This damages marine ecosystems, further reducing biodiversity. You can read more about soil erosion on page 16 – 17.

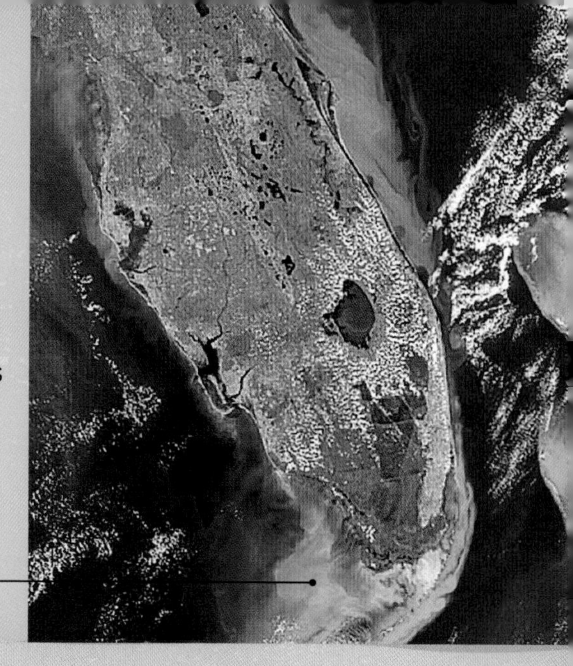

Soil running off into the ocean around Florida after a storm, seen from space.

SPOTLIGHT:

BIODIVERSITY

The variety of plant and animal life in a habitat is called biodiversity. A biodiverse habitat is more likely to be able to stay healthy overall, even if one species becomes extinct.

Habitats and humans

Healthy habitats aren't just important to the plants and animals that live in them. Supporting biodiversity through healthy habitats is important to human beings, too. We rely on flourishing forests to produce the oxygen that we breathe. We need many types of flying insects to pollinate our food crops (read more about the importance of pollinators on pages 24 – 25). We depend on natural vegetation to keep the soil stable, which prevents water pollution and flash flooding.

SOLVE IT!

FARM WITHOUT DEFORESTATION

Deforestation of the rainforest to grow coffee crops destroys animal habitats and depletes nutrients from the soil, but farmers need to grow crops to make a living. Look at the facts of the situation. Can you spot a solution that doesn't involve cutting down rainforest trees?

FACT ONE

Farmers chop down trees to grow coffee. But after a few years, the soil runs out of nutrients, and more rainforest trees are then cut down to find new, fertile soil to grow crops in.

FACT TWO

Rainforest trees are very tall! The top part of the tree is called the canopy.

FACT THREE

The rainforest canopy is a very important habitat. It is where many of the species that live in the rainforest find food, and make their homes.

CAN YOU SOLVE IT?

Taking into consideration the facts, how could the farmers improve their farming method?

Can you see a solution where:

- ▶ Farmers can still grow coffee to make a living?
- ▶ Farmers don't chop down more trees every few years to access new, fertile soil?
- ▶ Important rainforest habitats are preserved?

Draw and label your solution on a poster!

Still not sure? See page 42 for a solution.

TEST IT!

MIXED-VEG GARDEN PROJECT

You might not be able to grow a rainforest tree and a coffee bush where you live, but you can experiment with growing a mix of sun-loving and shade-loving food plants. Start this project in late spring.

YOU WILL NEED

a patch of soil, or a large, deep container with drainage holes in the bottom
compost
tomato and lettuce seeds
bamboo canes
string
scissors
a trowel
a tray
water
12 small pots or toilet roll tubes

STEP 1

Put four small pots or toilet roll tubes onto the tray and fill them with compost. Poke small holes in the compost a couple of centimeters deep using your finger.

STEP 2

Drop a couple of tomato seeds into the holes in each of the small pots. Cover all the seeds with compost, and water them until damp but not soaking wet.

STEP 3

Put the pots in a sheltered, sunny spot such as a windowsill and check that the soil is damp each day. After a few days, seedlings will appear. If both seeds in each pot sprout, remove the smaller one.

STEP 4

Once the seedlings are a few centimeters tall, you can ready them for planting into your garden or your container. Put the pots outside during the daytime and bring them in at night for a few days to help them adjust to the temperature.

STEP 5

Dig four holes in your large container or garden patch, the same depth as the small pot you have been growing your tomato seedlings in. Make sure they are at least 18 inches (45 cm) apart.

STEP 6

Tip the seedling and the soil out of the small pots and plant them in the holes. If using toilet rolls, just plant the whole tube, as it will break down in the soil. Press down the soil around the seedlings, and push a bamboo cane into the ground next to each seedling. Water them regularly.

STEP 7

When the tomato plants have got a bit taller, loosely tie them to the canes with string for extra support.

STEP 8

Next, sow eight pots with lettuce seeds in the same way. Plant the lettuces between and around the tomato plants. The tomato plants will grow tall and help shade the delicate lettuces. In a couple of months you'll have homegrown lettuces and tomatoes ready to eat.

THE ISSUE: SOIL EROSION

Many of us don't think about soil very much, and if we do it's just as something we accidentally bring indoors on our shoes. But soil is essential to our ability to grow food. Unfortunately, current farming practices are eroding our soil, which will create serious problems in the future.

Losing soil

As part of the processes of intensive agriculture, natural plants are removed from the land. The soil is ploughed to clear weeds, and add air and fertilizer. But during ploughing, and once the crops have been harvested, the soil is left bare. The topsoil gets blown away by wind and washed away by rain, and over time the layer of soil covering the land gets thinner and thinner.

Food in the future

As soil gets eroded, the land becomes less productive and the amount of food that can be grown on it goes down. Productivity is already declining around the world; in some countries very quickly. In Kenya, for example, productivity of croplands has dropped by 40 percent over the last 30 years. This threatens our ability to feed the Earth's growing population.

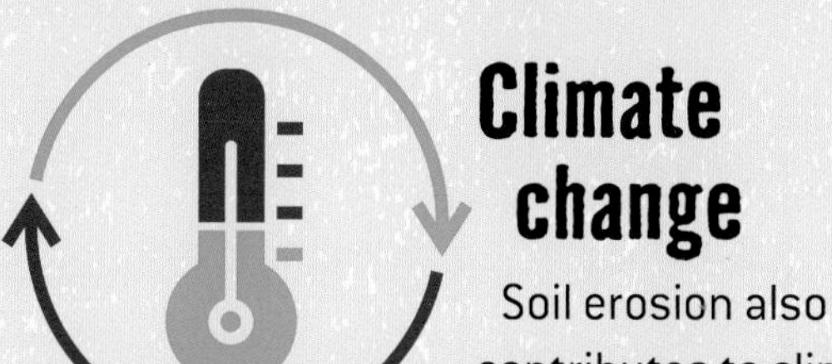

Climate change

Soil erosion also contributes to climate change. When plants grow, they take the greenhouse gas carbon dioxide out of the air. They use some of it to grow, and they also store some of it in the soil. If the soil is undisturbed it safely stores the carbon, away from the atmosphere. But when soils are eroded, they break down and release the carbon back into the atmosphere, making climate change worse.

Flooding

When soils are strong and healthy, they can help absorb rainwater. But when they are broken up by ploughing and are made thinner, they lose this ability. This means that in places with eroded soils, flash flooding after heavy rain is a risk to people's lives and properties.

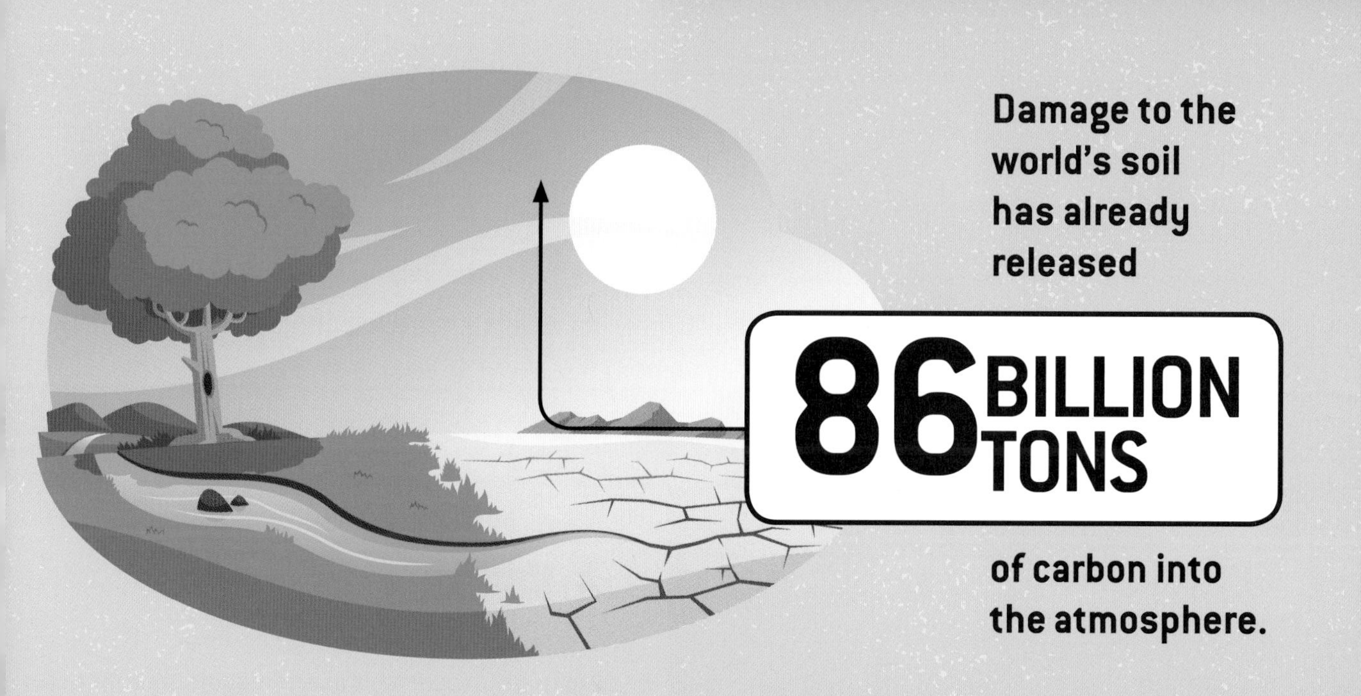

Damage to the world's soil has already released

86 BILLION TONS

of carbon into the atmosphere.

The good news is that there are ways to produce food and keep our soils healthy at the same time, and it all starts with an understanding of how soil is made.

UNDERSTANDING THE SOIL

Soil is a complex mixture of tiny bits of rock, decayed plant and animal matter, tiny bugs, fungi and bacteria, air and water. Soil plays a very important role in Earth's ecosystems, and there are many different types of soil depending on the exact mixture of rocks and organic material that it contains.

Sandy soils are crumbly and let water pass through easily. Clay soils are dense and hold onto more water.

SPOTLIGHT: SOIL FORMATION

Making new soil is a slow process. It takes several hundred years to form two centimeters of soil, so eroded soil cannot be quickly replaced.

A thin skin

Soil makes a thin layer that covers Earth's surface, a bit like the land's skin. The depth of the soil varies from place to place; in some areas it is only a couple of centimeters deep, in other areas it might reach a depth of six feet deep. As you dig down through the soil, you encounter different layers.

Lots of layers

The very surface of the soil is the organic layer. This part is purely organic material such as fallen leaves, twigs, and so on.

The topsoil is the second layer. It is the nutrient rich part of the soil that is good for growing plants. It contains a mixture of organic material and minerals from rocks.

Below the topsoil is subsoil, which is mostly made of rock particles or clay, as well as some minerals and organic material.

The parent material is a layer of broken-up rocks, which erode over time to help form the soil layers above.

The bottom layer is solid bedrock.

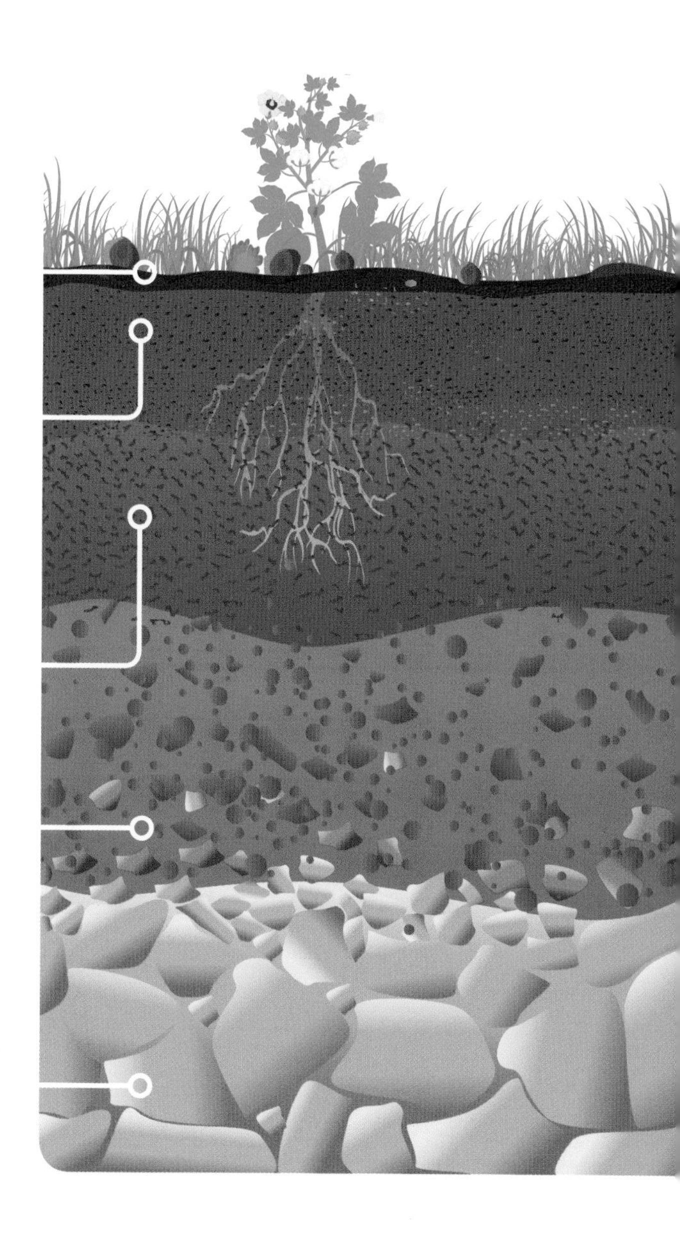

Stable soils

Soil can be crumbly and dry, or dense and heavy depending on the type of rock it is mostly made of. The amount of organic matter also makes a difference, as it acts a bit like a glue that keeps the soil together. When the soil is ploughed for agriculture, it breaks the soil up, and mixes more air in. This causes the organic matter to decay more, and means the soil holds together less well. Without that organic glue, the soil is more easily eroded.

SOLVE IT!

PROTECT THE SOIL

Ploughing the soil is mainly done to mix fertilizer into the soil and to dig up and kill weeds that are growing in it. However, ploughing also breaks down the soil, causing it to erode faster. Leaving fields bare after harvesting crops also leaves soil at risk of being washed away by rain. Experts have developed a way of allowing farmers to grow crops and protect their soil at the same time. Using these pieces of information, can you see how?

FACT ONE

Cash crops such as wheat and soya beans are planted in spring and harvested in autumn.

FACT TWO

It is possible to grow cover crops, such as rye or vetch, over winter as well as during the summer.

FACT THREE

An effective way to stop weeds growing is to use a mulch. This is a layer of material (such as straw or other plant material) put on top of the soil to stop weeds growing by blocking their light.

FACT FOUR

Natural mulches made from plants can also enrich the soil as they rot down, in just the same way that soil stays fertile in natural ecosystems.

FACT FIVE

When plants are growing on the land, they stop rain and wind from carrying the soil away.

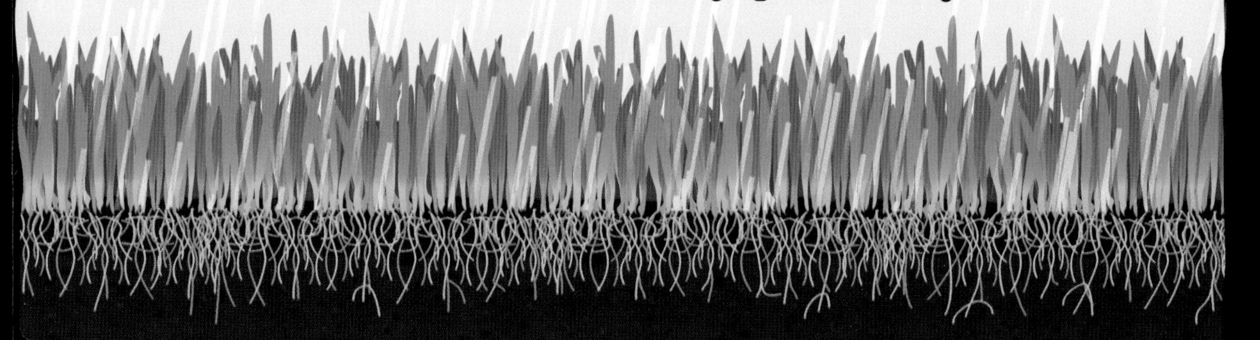

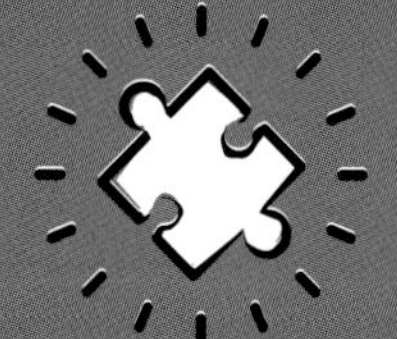

CAN YOU SOLVE IT?

Think about each of these pieces of information. Bare soil allows erosion, so how can a farmer keep the soil covered? How does nature return nutrients, which crops can use, back to the soil?

- What effect does keeping the ground covered have on unwanted weeds?
- Write a plan for the farmer. List what to grow in each season, and what to do with the plants afterwards to protect the soil.

Still not sure? See page 43 for a solution.

TEST IT!

SOIL EROSION EXPERIMENT

See soil erosion in action and try out some ways to prevent it with this experiment. Ask an adult for help cutting the plastic bottles if you need.

YOU WILL NEED

6 plastic half-gallon (2-liter) bottles
scissors
4 small potted plants, such as basil plants
a few handfuls of straw
a mixture of garden soil and potting compost
string
water
measuring jug
duct tape

STEP 1

Cut a large rectangular hole out of the side of three of the bottles. This makes them into a basic planter shape.

STEP 2

Use duct tape to secure the bottles to a table or other surface so they don't roll around. The necks of the bottles should overhang the edge of the table.

STEP 3

Fill each of the three bottles with a mixture of soil and potting compost. Leave one of the bottles with bare soil. Cover the soil in the second bottle with a thick layer of straw. Press the straw down so it lays flat.

STEP ④

Cut the top half off the remaining three bottles and discard them, leaving you with three small plastic buckets. Poke two holes opposite each other in the rim of each bucket.

STEP ⑤

Plant your four plants closely together in the third bottle. Press the soil down firmly around them to bed them in. You want to create the effect of a thickly grown field of plants.

STEP ⑥

Make a string handle for each bucket by threading a length of string through the two holes and tying knots at the ends. Hang these buckets from the necks of the planter bottles, off the edge of the table.

STEP ⑦

Using the measuring jug, pour an equal amount of water into each planter bottle. Observe the colour of the water that runs out of the bottle necks and into the buckets below. How much soil has been washed out of each bottle? What does this tell you about the best ways to prevent soil erosion?

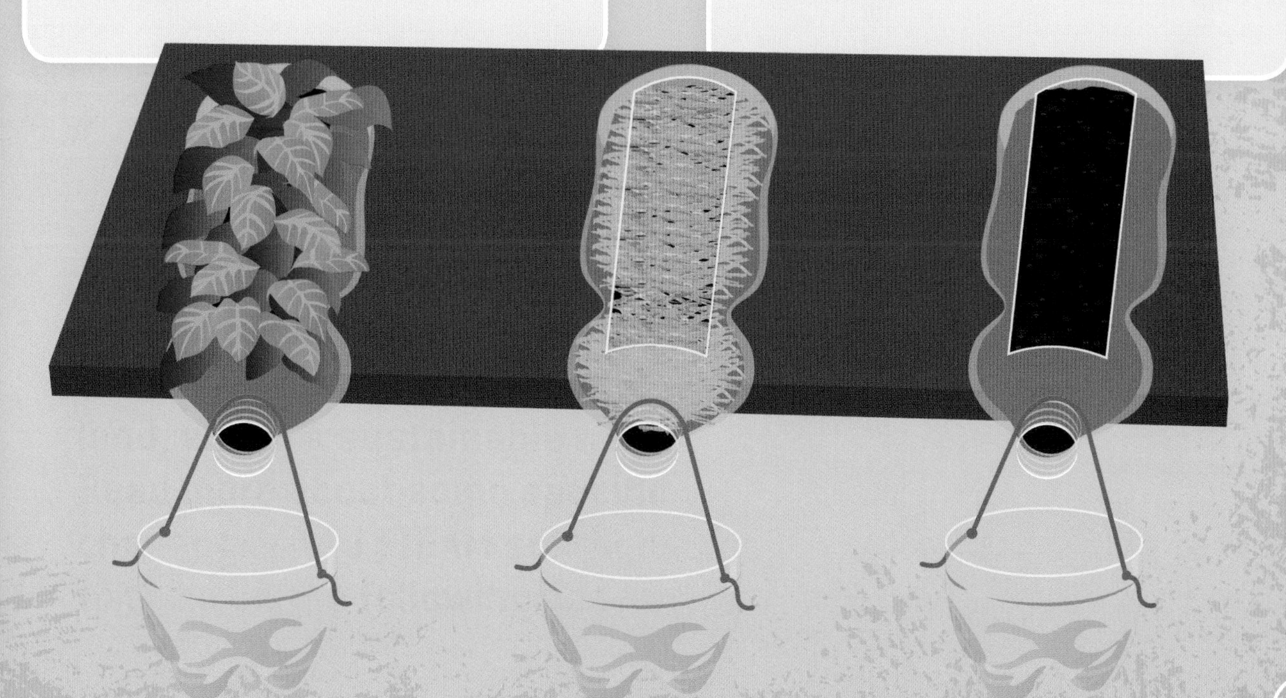

THE ISSUE:

POLLINATORS UNDER THREAT

Do you like strawberries? How about apples, pears, peaches, chocolate, tea, or coffee? Did you know that over three-quarters of our fruits, vegetables, and nuts need to be pollinated by insects such as bees and flies to grow? Unfortunately, current farming methods are seriously endangering bees, butterflies and other flying insects.

Essential insects

Flying insects are a very important part of Earth's ecosystems. They support many food chains, feeding wildlife such as birds and bats, which then go on to provide food for bigger predators such as owls or foxes. They also play a hugely important role in pollinating plants, which provide food for other insects, birds, and animals. Unfortunately, flying insect numbers have declined massively in the last 25 years.

Feeding us

As well as supporting natural ecosystems, we rely on flying insects to feed us humans, too. Flying insects are the key pollinators that help our crops to grow fruit and seeds. If pollinators were to disappear altogether, we would not be able to feed ourselves.

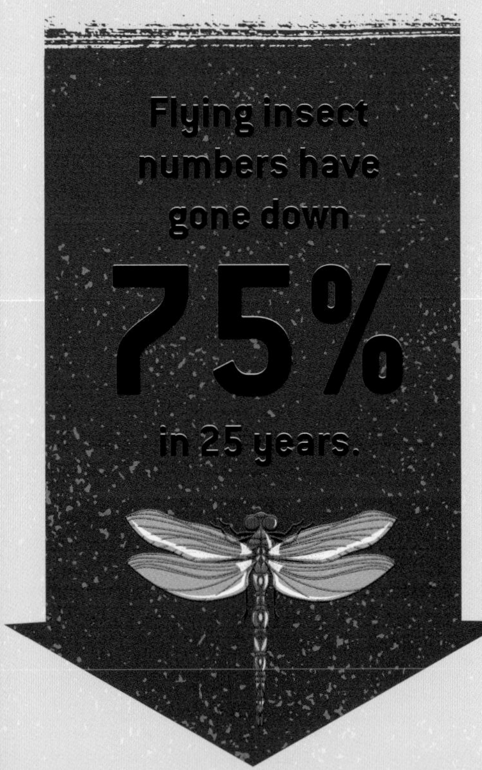

Habitat loss

There are several ways that current agricultural practices are driving down pollinator numbers. The first is habitat loss. In intensively farmed monoculture areas, there is no food for the flying insects to eat. Flying insects need wildflowers to provide a source of nectar and pollen to feed on throughout the year. In intensively farmed areas, all the native wildflowers are cleared, and crop plants only provide nectar and pollen at certain times of the year.

Pesticide poisoning

Another problem for pollinators has been created by the widespread use of pesticides. In monoculture areas, insect pests that eat and damage crops can balloon in number, because the natural predators for those pests have been removed along with the rest of the natural ecosystem. To address this, farmers use pesticides to control their numbers. But pesticides can often harm the helpful pollinator species, too.

SPOTLIGHT: PESTICIDES

Pesticides are chemicals that are sprayed onto crops to kill off pests. However, pesticides can also have negative impacts on human health and the health of the surrounding ecosystems.

PLANTS, POLLINATORS, AND ECOSYSTEMS

Have you ever seen a bumblebee, its fuzzy hairs covered with yellow or orange dust as it buzzes from flower to flower? Bees and other insects visit flowers to drink nectar and collect pollen for their larvae. As they do so, they fertilize the plants they visit by accidentally carrying pollen between them.

Flowers

Plants grow flowers especially to attract pollinating insects. The bright colors of the petals and the sweet scent of the flowers send a signal to passing bees, butterflies and other insects that there is energy rich nectar inside. In this way, the plants and the insects rely on one another for food and reproduction.

A single bee can visit up to 5,000 flowers in one day.

Producing fruit

Pollen is produced by the male part of the flower, the anther. When pollen is carried to another flower by a bee or other insect, it is received by the female parts. It sticks to the stigma and moves down to the ovary, where it fertilizes the ovules which develop into seeds. The ovary turns into the fruit, but only if it has been pollinated. Without pollination, the plant can't make any fruit.

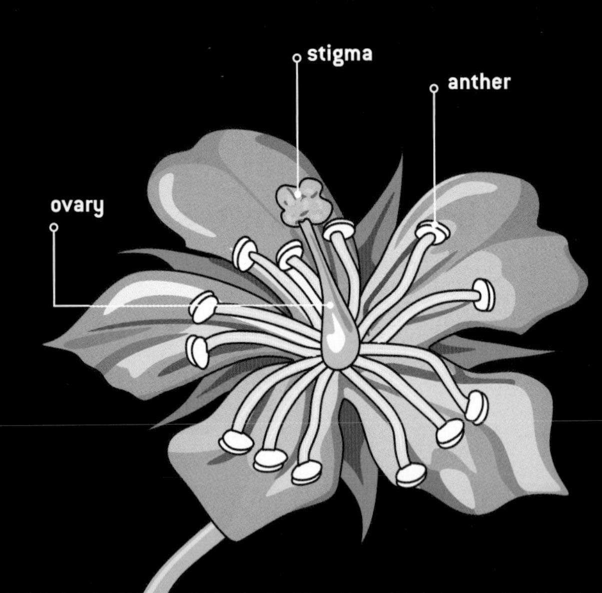

Insect pests

Pollinators aren't the only creatures that visit crops for their food. Some insects, such as caterpillars and aphids, eat the leaves or the sticky sap inside the plants' stems, which damages plants grown for humans to eat. In the wild, the numbers of these insects are kept down by predators as part of the natural balancing effect of a healthy ecosystem.

SPOTLIGHT: PREDATORY INSECTS

Some insect species including ladybugs, lacewings, and parasitic wasps eat other small insects such as aphids and caterpillars.

ladybug

lacewing

Working together

An ecosystem is just that – an ecological system that works together. It includes all the living and non-living things in a particular area, such as the plants, animals, water, and soil. A healthy ecosystem supports itself, and the only input it needs is energy from the sun. All the other nutrients and water are cycled around the system, and each species has a role to play – as predator or prey – in keeping the other parts of the ecosystem in balance.

SOLVE IT!

POLLINATOR-FRIENDLY FARMING

In current monocultural farming systems, pollinators can be too few in number and pests can get out of control. At the same time, the pesticides used to kill unwanted insects can end up harming helpful pollinators. Some apple farmers are already using a method that supports pollinators while also reducing the number of pests. Can you see how to do it?

FACT ONE

Apple trees need to be pollinated in order to produce apples.

FACT TWO

Bees and other pollinators need wildflowers to provide a year-round source of food.

FACT THREE

Aphids are a common apple tree pest.

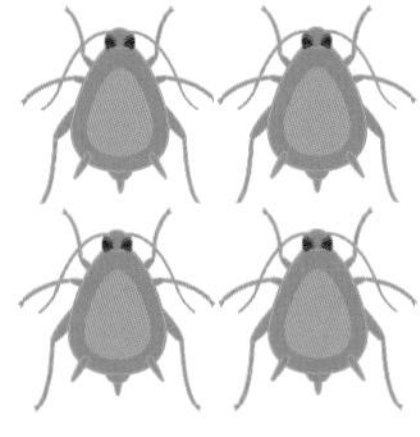

FACT FOUR

Predatory insects such as lacewings and ladybugs eat aphids.

FACT FIVE

Pollinators and predatory insects live and nest in vegetation such as tall grasses, trees, fallen branches, and hedges.

TEST IT! INSECT SURVEY

Discover which types of habitat contain the most insect biodiversity by making your own home-made insect-trapping device called a pooter.

YOU WILL NEED

small clear plastic tub with a lid
scissors
flexible drinking straw, the wider the better
small piece of nylon tights material
elastic band
plasticine
tape measure

STEP ①

Poke a hole in the center of the lid and in the center of the bottom of the plastic container using the scissors. Ask an adult for help if you need it.

STEP ②

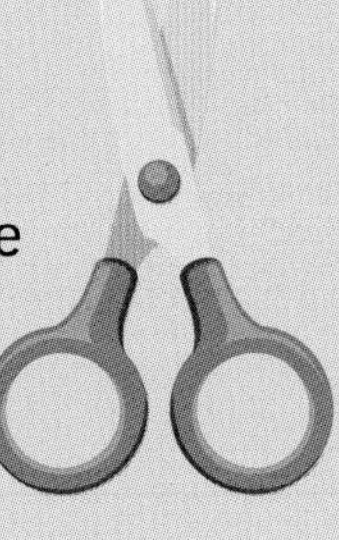

Snip the holes so they are the same size as the straw. Snip a 2.4 inch (6 cm)-long piece from the bottom of the straw, and keep it.

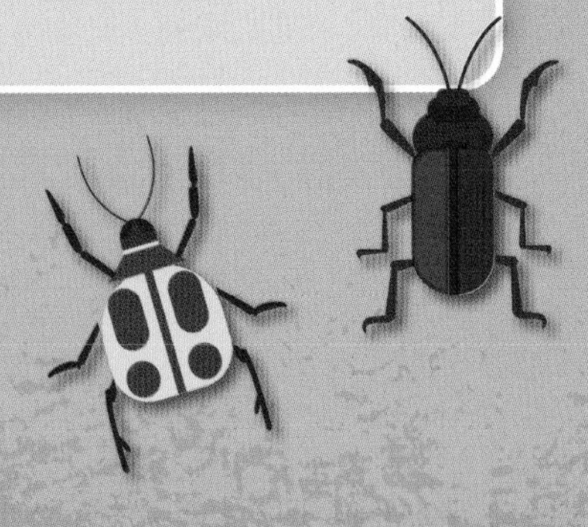

STEP ③

Cover the end of the bendy length of straw with the piece of tights material, and hold it in place with the elastic band.

STEP ④

Push the 2.4 inch (6 cm)-piece of straw into the hole in the bottom of the container so that it pokes out, and seal around the edge between the straw and the pot with plasticine.

STEP ⑤

Push the bendy piece of straw through the hole in the lid, so that the material-covered end sits inside the container and the flexible part pokes out of the top.

STEP ⑥

Seal around the straw with plasticine and put the lid on the container.

STEP ⑦

To catch insects with your pooter, hold the end of the short straw over any insect you spot and suck on the longer straw. The insect will be sucked inside the pot where you can identify it.

STEP ⑧

Take your pooter to different areas, such as a hedgerow, a grassy park, a patch of trees, and so on. See how many insects you can find and identify within a foot-square area at each spot. Which areas have the most insects? Which have the greatest variety? Carefully release any insects you capture back into the wild afterwards.

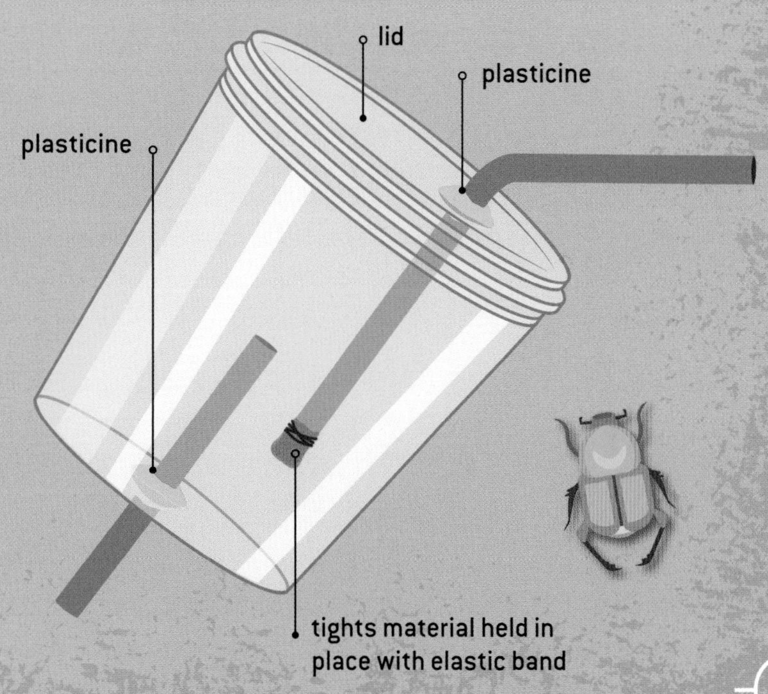

THE ISSUE:

LOST PLANT VARIETY

Think of a banana. What color is it? What does it taste like? You can probably answer that exactly. Now think of an apple. What color is it? Is it sweet or sharp? Those are questions with several answers – because, unlike bananas, we see lots of different types of apple on the supermarket shelves. There are red ones, green ones, sweet ones, and sharp ones. We see a lot of apple varieties, but we don't see a lot of banana varieties. Lack of variety is an issue across our food system.

SPOTLIGHT: BANANAS

Bananas actually come in hundreds of varieties, and in many colors and sizes, just like apples. But 95 percent of the bananas exported around the world are a single variety called the Cavendish.

Identical stock

At the beginning of the twentieth century, there were hundreds of different varieties of lettuce, tomato, and sqash that were grown and sold commercially by greengrocers. But since supermarkets and industrial monocrop agriculture took over, the number of varieties sold has been greatly reduced. Walk into any supermarket and the varieties of fruits and veggies on sale will be largely the same.

Insecure system

You might wonder, what's the big deal with having fewer varieties? The problem is that, just like in a natural ecosystem, biodiversity is what makes a system healthy and sustainable. For example, if a new disease were to affect the Cavendish banana variety, most of the world's banana supply would disappear. In a world where the climate is changing quickly, having a lot of different types is key to ensuring there are always varieties that can withstand new climate conditions or resist disease.

Over the twentieth century, 75 percent of food plant varieties became extinct.

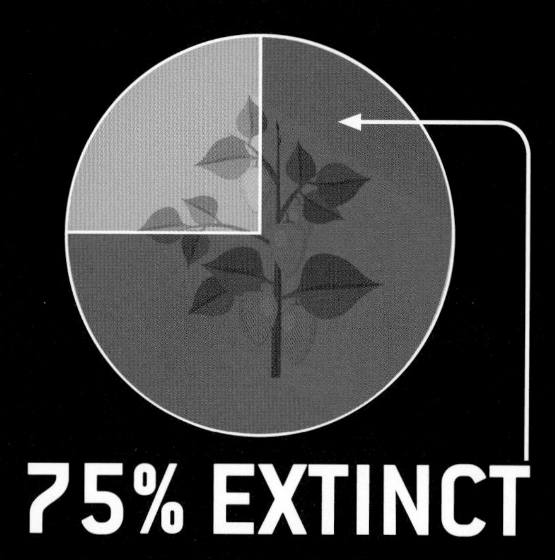

Wheat and corn

Lack of biodiversity is an issue with wheat and corn crops too. Most industrially farmed grain crops are grown from seeds that are developed by seed companies to be as uniform as possible. In the past, farmers grew varieties that were adapted to local conditions. For example, in a rainy area, the local variety would be adapted to heavy rainfall. In a dry area, the local variety could withstand drought. Now that the climate is changing fast, it is important to preserve and develop varieties that can deal with the changing weather.

EVOLUTION AND INHERITANCE

Do you look like either of your parents? Perhaps you have your dad's nose, or the same color eyes as your mom. The reason for these similarities is genetic inheritance: the way that physical traits are passed on from parents to offspring. Plants also inherit characteristics from their parents.

Useful traits

Evolution also explains how different types of plant and animal can develop. Living things move around: animals move, and plants spread their seeds. The traits that are useful in one place might not be useful in another area. For example, as a plant spreads from land covered in soil to a sandy beach, it will benefit from developing deeper roots to help it stay anchored in shifting, sandy ground.

SPOTLIGHT: EVOLUTION

Evolution causes living things to change over time. It happens through what is known as natural selection: living things that are better suited to their environment are able to survive and have more offspring, and so they pass on the traits that make them successful.

Artificial selection

Humans can speed up this process of natural selection with artificial selection, or breeding. They can save the seeds from the hardiest plants or the juiciest fruit to make sure that next year's crop has those traits. Or, they can pollinate a hardy plant with a plant that has juicy fruit to try and create offspring that have both of those traits.

Breeding and biodiversity

Humans have been breeding food plants for desirable traits for thousands of years. This is why almost everything we eat is very different to its wild relatives. People breeding plants that are adapted well to the local environment is what gave us a huge diversity of food plant varieties in the first place. However, breeding can also reduce biodiversity as well as improve it.

Risks

When plants or animals are bred to enhance one particular trait (such as more grains in a wheat plant), breeders will often create offspring from closely related parents. This reduces the amount of genetic diversity in the offspring. It is risky, because if a new disease arrives, the whole population could be wiped out if no individuals have a gene making them resistant to it.

SOLVE IT!

CLIMATE-PROOF FARMING

In the future, weather patterns around the world will change. Some areas will see increased drought, while others will start to receive more rainfall. A sustainable food system that can adapt well to changes involves having a wide variety of crops. So what should farmers, shoppers and scientists be doing to make sure our food systems are safe?

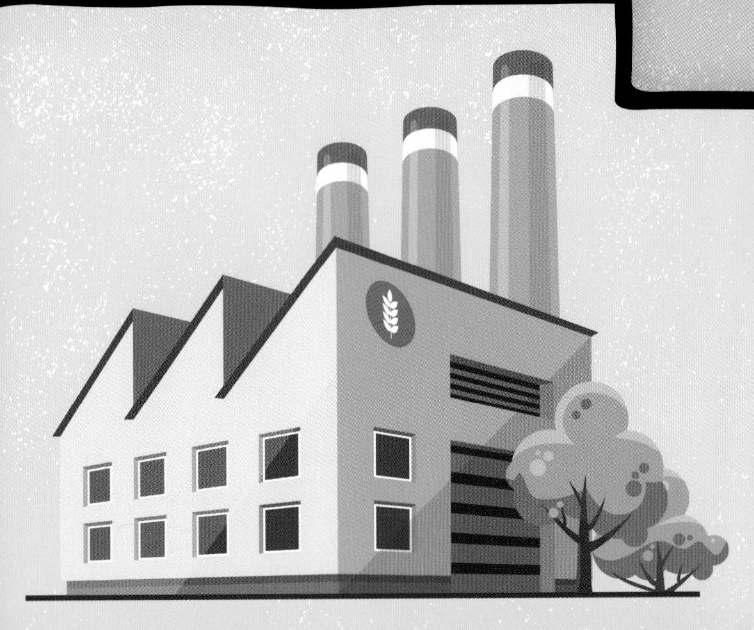

FACT ONE

Large seed companies develop and sell seeds. Scientists working for them have funding for large-scale research, but often focus on creating uniform seeds.

FACT TWO

Farmers can save the seeds of many varieties of crops to grow them again and breed them. However, they are legally not allowed to do this with seeds bought from large companies.

FACT THREE

Farmers buying seeds from large companies often grow one type of crop over a very large area. The farmer is reliant on this one crop and it may only grow well in particular weather conditions.

FACT FOUR

Shoppers buy a lot of their food from supermarkets, which are often stocked with limited varieties of fruit and vegetables. Less popular versions of crops, not sold by big seed companies, can go extinct because people don't want to buy them. Grocers, farmers' markets, and veg box schemes often have a much greater variety of produce.

TEST IT!

HEIRLOOM TOMATO TRIALS

Old varieties of edible crops are called heritage or heirloom varieties. Starting in early spring, try growing a couple of different types of heirloom tomatoes in different growing conditions.

YOU WILL NEED

- 2 tomato grow bags or deep containers of equivalent size with drainage holes
- compost
- a trowel
- 6 small pots or toilet-roll tubes
- a tray
- water
- bamboo canes
- string
- scissors
- 2 types of heirloom tomato seeds (available online)
- liquid tomato feed

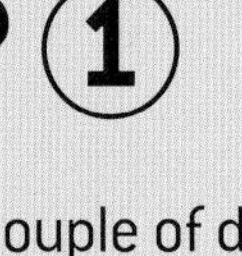

STEP 1

Choose a couple of different heirloom tomato varieties that look interesting to you. Perhaps a purple variety, or even a white variety? You can find heirloom tomato seed stores by searching online.

STEP 2

Start off your seeds in the small pots or toilet-roll tubes. Fill the pots or tubes with compost, place them on the tray and make holes for the seeds using your finger.

STEP 3

Plant half of your pots with one variety, and the other half with your second variety. Put a couple of seeds in each pot in case one seed doesn't sprout, and cover with compost.

STEP ④

Water your seeds and put them on a sunny, sheltered windowsill. Observe your pots to see which variety produces seedlings the quickest. Plants that mature faster can withstand pests and diease better.

STEP ⑤

When your seedlings are a few centimeters high, put them outside only during the daytime for a few days. Next, replant them outside in the large containers or grow bags. In order to test how well the plants survive in different conditions, plant half of each variety in each container. Stake them with bamboo canes for support.

STEP ⑥

Give one of your containers water less often than the other. Watch to see what effect this has on the plants. Does one type of tomato do better than the other under different watering conditions?

STEP ⑦

Give your plants regular doses of liquid tomato feed. Watch to see which variety grows the fastest. Does one produce tomatoes sooner? When your tomatoes are ripe, harvest them and do a taste test. Which variety do you think has the better flavor?

FARMING IN THE FUTURE

As governments, farmers, citizens and big international organizations around the world increasingly realize that the way we are currently farming is not sustainable, we will start to see more and more changes in the way food is grown. Here are a few of the innovations people are already using and working on to address the changing climate and increased demand for food.

Desert technology

How do you grow crops in the desert? Desalination, which is removing salt from seawater, is being used in areas of Australia that have been suffering from drought. Desalination is a very energy intensive process, so using fossil fuel energy to do it is not environmentally friendly. However, in hot, sunny regions it is possible to use solar energy to power the process instead: creating fresh water to grow plants in dry areas.

Ocean farms

It isn't necessary to take the salt out of seawater if the plants you are growing are adapted for it. Already used in Asian cooking, some people think seaweed should become a more important part of everyone's diet. Thousands of edible plants from the ocean could be farmed in a sustainable way. They are high in vitamin C, calcium, protein, and omega-3 oils, and a lot of crops can be grown in a small area. Ocean plants can also help reduce climate change by taking carbon out of the atmosphere.

Perennial crops

Another group of scientists is attempting to make food crops that are more climate-friendly by developing perennial food plants. The majority of our staple food crops such as wheat and rice are annuals. This means the whole plant grows and is harvested in one year. A perennial crop would live for several years and be repeatedly harvested. Perennial crops don't have to be replanted every year, meaning they protect the soil. They can compete better with weed plants, so herbicides are not needed.

of our calories currently come from annual crops.

Farming the city

As more and more of the global population move from the countryside to cities, it makes sense to grow food where people live. But how do you grow food efficiently when space is at a premium? Vertical farming systems stack racks of plants inside, and grow them using artificial lighting and hydroponic methods. This sort of indoor farming can be used to grow food year-round, on very little land.

ANSWERS

SOLVE IT! FARM WITHOUT DEFORESTATION PAGES 12–13

A way to farm coffee and cocoa, while also helping to preserve natural habitat, is through shade-growing. Coffee and cocoa bushes can be planted beneath the tall rainforest trees, instead of cutting them down. This preserves bird habitat, provides soil protection, increases carbon storage, provides natural pest control and improves pollination.

Agroforestry

Growing crops underneath trees instead of deforesting an area is called agroforestry. It can provide other benefits to the farmers, as well as to wildlife. In rainforest areas, farmers can get additional income from ecotourism. Building materials, firewood and medicinal plants can also be harvested from the forest when done sustainably.

SOLVE IT! PROTECT THE SOIL PAGES 20–21

In the wild, new plants grow without the soil being ploughed. By copying nature, farmers are able to grow crops without breaking up the soil or using lots of herbicides to kill weeds. The system works like this:

Spring
The farmer plants the cash crop, such as wheat or soya beans.

Summer
The cash crop grows during the summer, taking advantage of the sunshine.

Autumn
The cash crop is harvested. The stalks of the wheat or beans are left in the ground. A cover crop such as rye or vetch is planted straight into the ground among the stalks.

Winter
The cover crop grows over winter, ensuring the soil is protected.

Spring
The following spring, the cover crop is either mown or simply crushed flat onto the ground, creating a mulch. The new season's cash crop is planted straight into thin channels cut in the mulch. Because the rest of the ground is covered, weeds don't grow to compete with the cash crop.

ANSWERS

SOLVE IT! POLLINATOR-FRIENDLY FARMING PAGES 28–29

A healthy farm has a natural mix of pollinators and predatory insects to help the crops grow and protect them from pests. Farmers can encourage these kinds of insects onto their farm by planting wildflowers, tall grasses and hedgerows around the edges of their fields and among their crops.

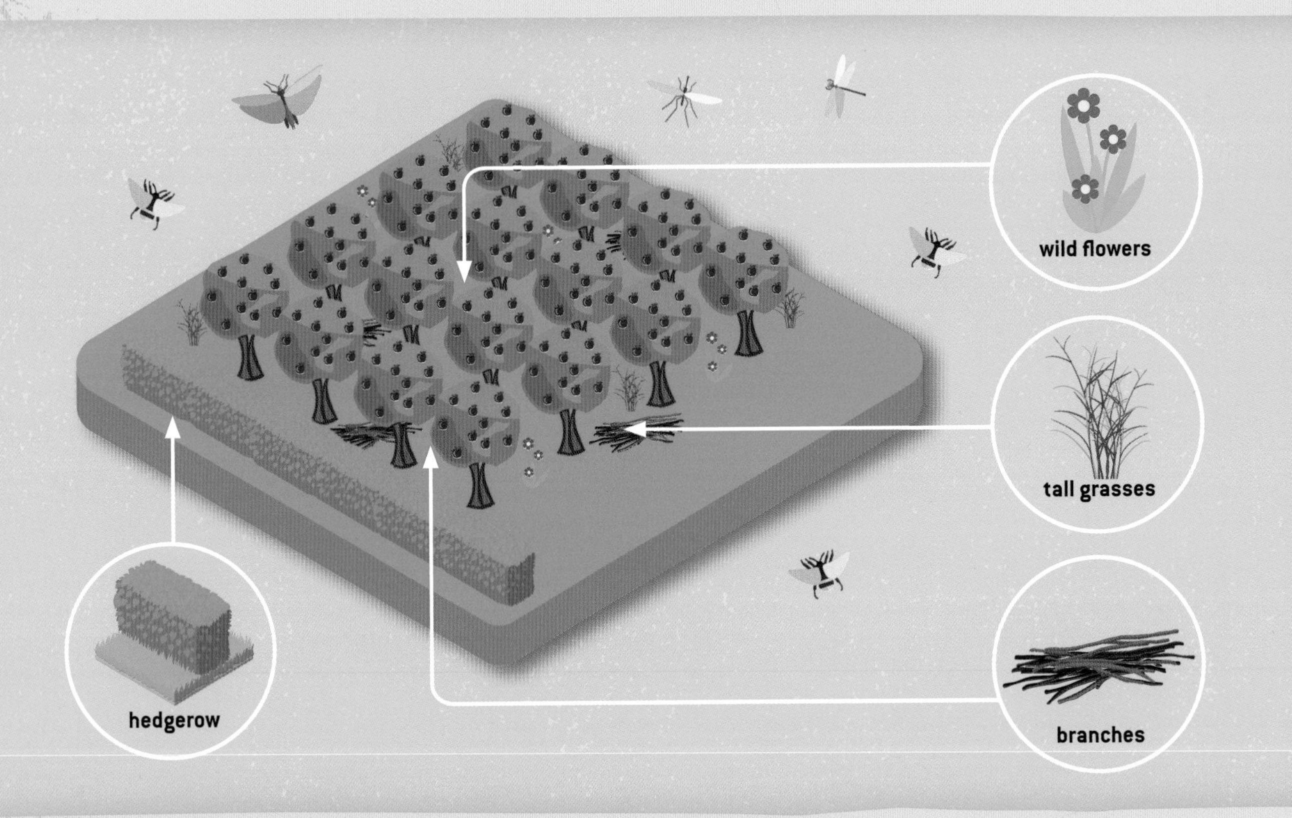

Underplanting

By underplanting wildflowers through an orchard, as well as growing hedgerows around the edges and leaving piles of natural brushwood, the apple farmer can provide habitat and year-round food for pollinators. Farmers growing any type of crop can apply this approach, as it doesn't only benefit insects. The soil is strengthed by having strips of natural vegetation, and water runoff is also reduced.

SOLVE IT! CLIMATE-PROOF FARMING PAGES 36–37

By changing the crops we buy, grow and develop, we can ensure there is enough variety in our food systems to prepare for the effects of climate change.

Scientists and researchers at big seed companies can help by researching and enhancing crop diversity. For example, in an area where climate change is expected to bring drier weather, scientists can research which crop varieties are thriving in dry areas of the world. They can also explore the options for breeding from those dry-adapted plants to evolve even stronger varieties.

Farmers can help by sourcing and growing different varieties of crops, rather than buying a single crop from a large seed company. Then they can save seeds to grow again and breed new varieties to ensure there is always a diversity of crops available. They can also share seeds with other farmers to increase their crop diversity.

Shoppers can help by trying unfamiliar kinds of fruits and vegetables and showing that different varieties can sell well. They can also buy directly from growers through farmers' markets and veg box schemes instead of from the supermarket. This ensures that farmers can afford to keep growing different types of fruit and vegetables.

PUTTING IT ALL TOGETHER

If you think about the environmentally friendly, sustainable STEAM solutions in this book, what do you notice about what they have in common? They all take their lead from nature one way or another. There is a word for this: agroecology. Agroecology is the science of applying ecological concepts and principles to the design, development, and management of agricultural systems.

Helping out

Even if you aren't a farmer or agroecologist, you can still help solve these issues in other ways. Ask your parents to buy organically grown food from a local farmers' market, or look out for rainforest-friendly chocolate in the shops. You can also support pollinators by planting wildflowers in your garden or in a window box, or by starting a project at school to plant them on school grounds.

GLOSSARY

adaptation a special ability or physical trait that helps an animal to survive

agriculture the practice of preparing the soil and growing crops or raising animals for food

annual (crop) a plant that grows, flowers and dies all within one year

artificial selection the deliberate breeding of plants or animals to create offspring with desirable traits

biodiversity the variety of plants and animals

cash crop a crop that farmers grow specifically to sell in exchange for money

climate change the changes in world weather patterns caused by human activity

desalination a process that removes salt from seawater

ecosystem all of the living things, such as plants and animals, and the non-living things, such as rocks, in a particular area

ecotourism tourism focused around watching wildlife or helping conservation efforts

emissions something that has been released or put out into the world, such as gases from a car exhaust

evolution the idea that all living things have changed over time, and that new species develop from earlier types

fertilizer a substance added to the soil to provide the nutrients that help plants grow

finite having a limited amount

flash flood a sudden, local flood, usually after heavy rain

food chain the order in which living things eat one another, starting with plants and finishing with large predators

fossil fuel a fuel such as oil or coal that was formed over millions of years from dead plants and animals

gene a microscopic instruction in a living thing's cells that determine things such as how it will look

global warming the gradual warming of the Earth's atmosphere and oceans caused by human activity

greengrocer a shop selling fruits and vegetables

greenhouse gas a gas in the Earth's atmosphere that traps heat from the sun, gradually causing the Earth to warm up

herbicide a chemical that is used to kill unwanted plants such as weeds

hydroponics a method for growing fruits and vegetables without soil, using nutrients dissolved in water

larvae the young of insects such as bees

monoculture the practice of growing or producing a single type of crop plant or livestock animal over a large area

mulch a layer of material such as straw or dead plant material that is laid on the ground to stop weeds from growing by blocking light to the soil, and to slowly improve the nutrient levels in the soil as it rots down

nutrients substances that living things need for healthy growth

organic material matter that has recently come from a living thing, such as fallen leaves, dead plants or animals or animal dung

perennial (crop) a plant that lasts for several seasons. It grows, produces flowers and fruits which can be harvested, and survives to complete the cycle several times before dying

pesticide a chemical used to kill off unwanted insects

pollinator a plant or animal that carries pollen between plants, helping them to produce fruit and reproduce

pooter a small jar for collecting and identifying insects

productivity the amount of crops that can be grown in an area of land. Productivity is affected by factors such as the amount of nutrients in the soil

sustainable any practice that can be carried out continuously without using up natural resources or causing harm to the environment

INDEX